PIANO SOLO

GALACTIC THEMES

ISBN 978-1-5400-0369-0

HAL•LEONARD®
7777 W. BLUEMOUND RD. P.O. BOX 13819 MILWAUKEE, WI 53213

Visit Hal Leonard Online at
www.halleonard.com

ALL SYSTEMS GO
from APOLLO 13

Composed by
JAMES HORNER

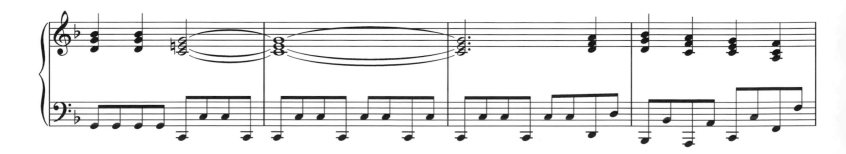

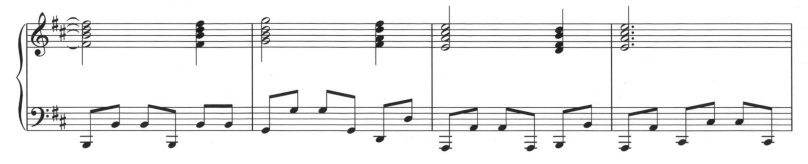

ALSO SPRACH ZARATHUSTRA

featured in the Motion Picture 2001: A SPACE ODYSSEY

By RICHARD STRAUSS

Moderately

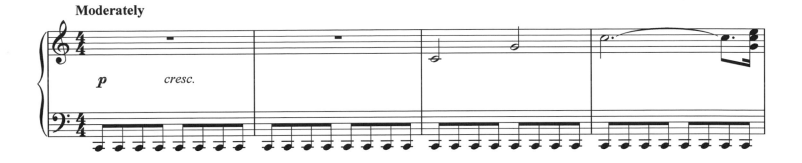

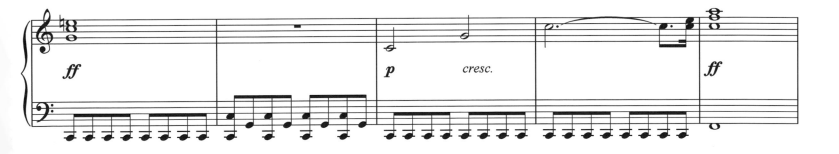

THEME FROM ARMAGEDDON

from ARMAGEDDON

Music by TREVOR RABIN

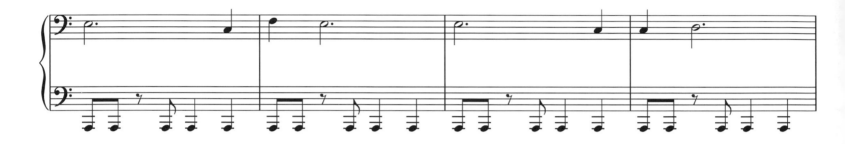

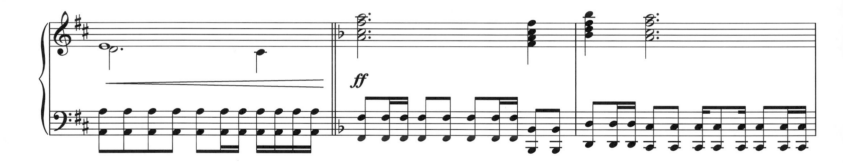

THEME FROM CLOSE ENCOUNTERS OF THE THIRD KIND

By JOHN WILLIAMS

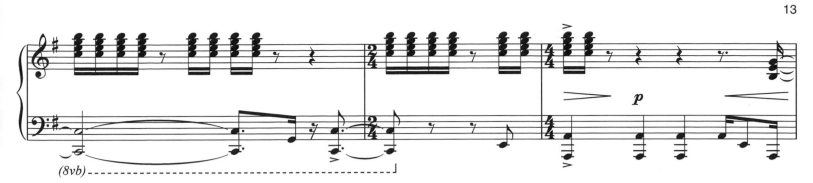

BATTLESTAR GALACTICA
Theme from the Universal Television Series BATTLESTAR GALACTICA

By STU PHILLIPS
and GLEN LARSON

Majestically

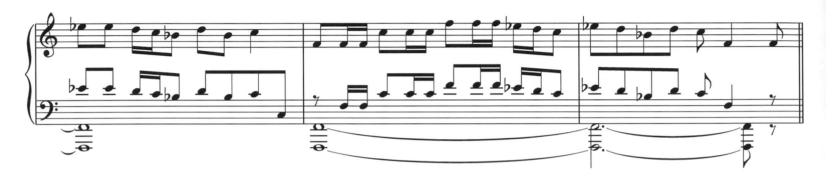

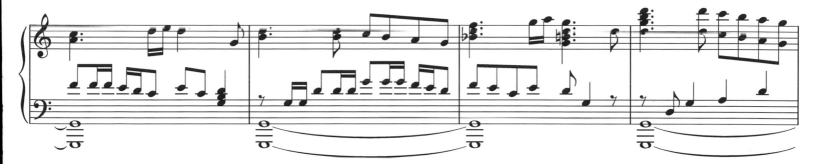

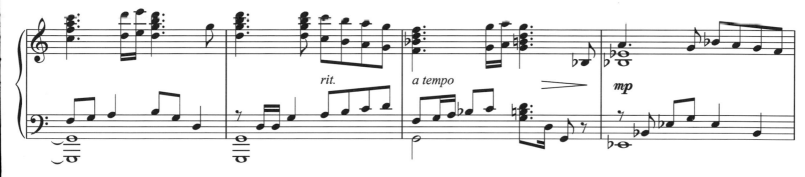

DOCTOR WHO

By RON GRAINER

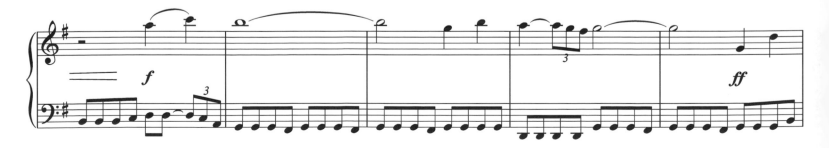

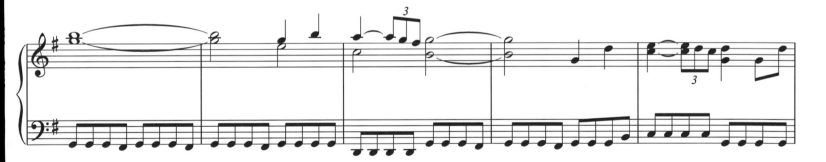

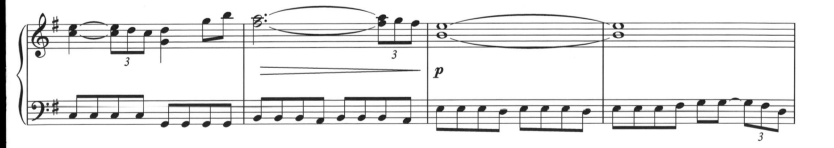

THEME FROM E.T.
(The Extra-Terrestrial)
from the Universal Picture E.T. (THE EXTRA-TERRESTRIAL)

Music by JOHN WILLIAMS

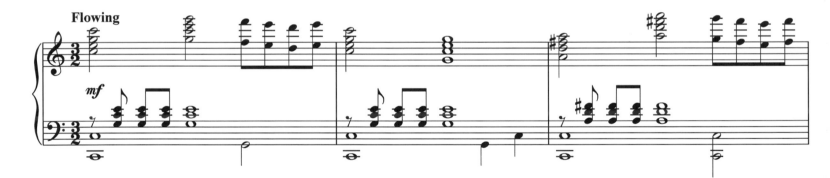

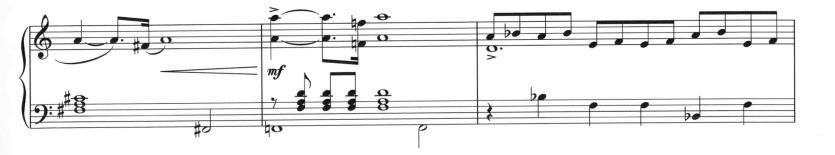

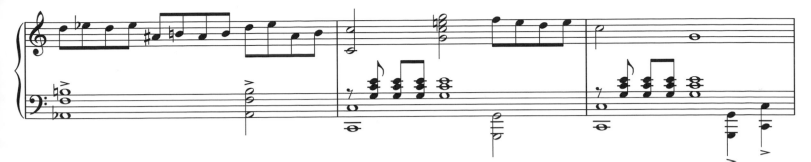

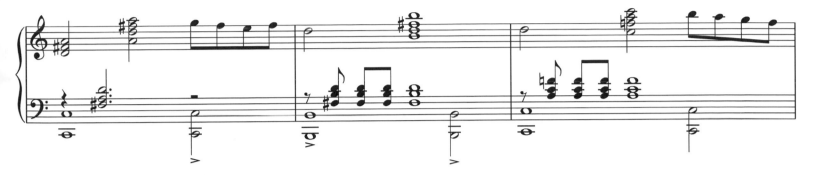

Meno mosso (in 3)

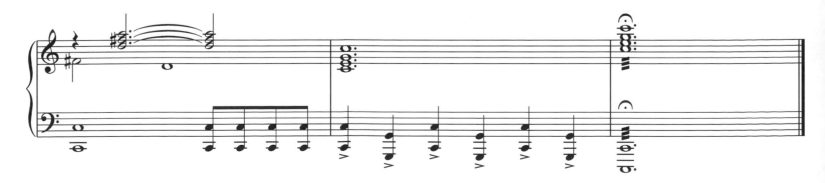

FIREFLY MAIN TITLE

Composed by
JOSS WHEDON

Moderately

FIRST STEP
from the Paramount Pictures film INTERSTELLAR

By HANS ZIMMER,
RYAN RUBIN and ALEX GIBSON

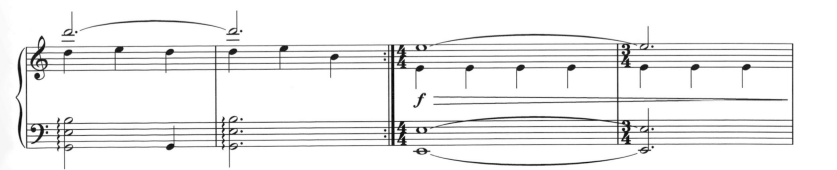

26

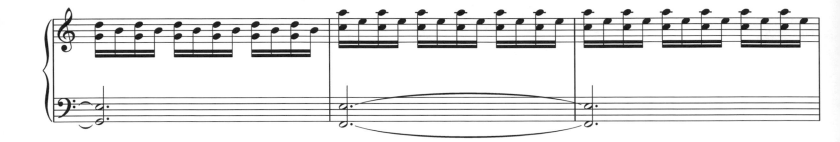

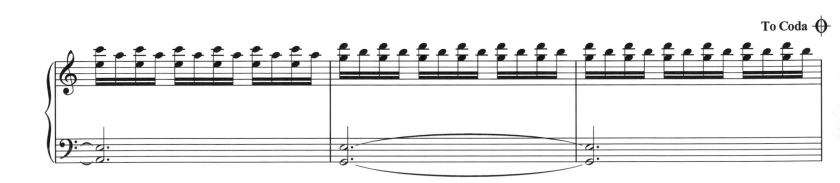

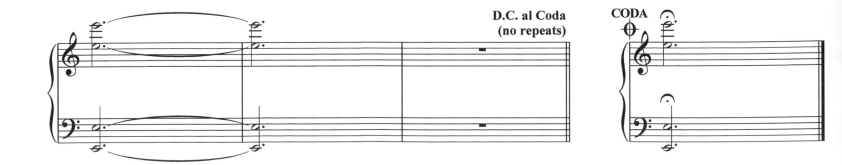

THE HUNT
from PLANET OF THE APES

By JERRY GOLDSMITH

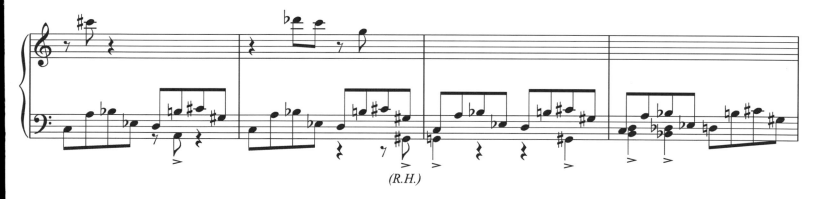

GUARDIANS INFERNO
from GUARDIANS OF THE GALAXY VOL. 2

Words and Music by JAMES GUNN
and TYLER BATES

Disco beat

To Coda ⊕

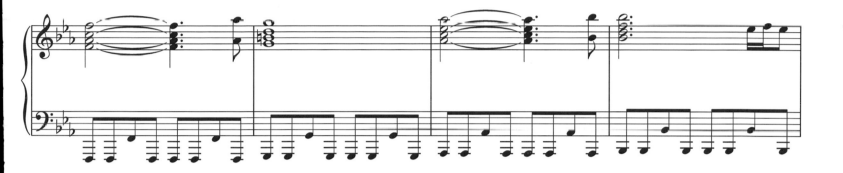

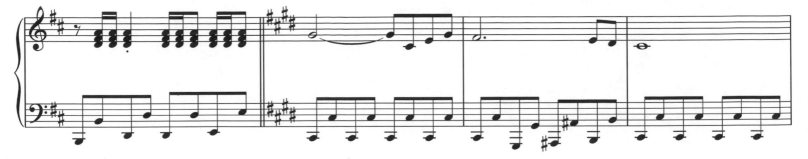

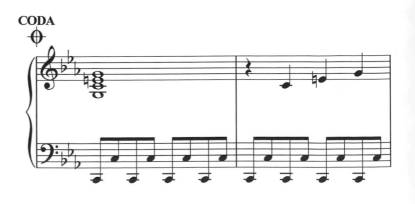

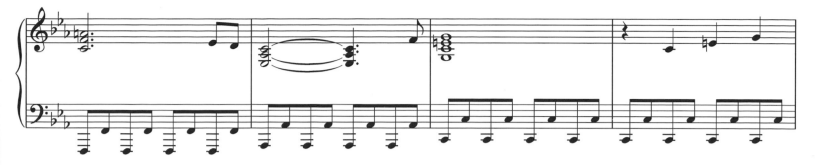

Slow and majestic

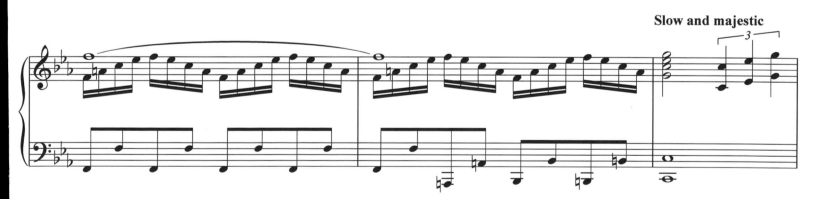

I SEE YOU
(Theme from AVATAR)
from the Twentieth Century Fox Motion Picture AVATAR

Lyrics by SIMON FRANGLEN,
JAMES HORNER and KUK HARRELL
Music by JAMES HORNER and SIMON FRANGLEN

Slowly, dramatically

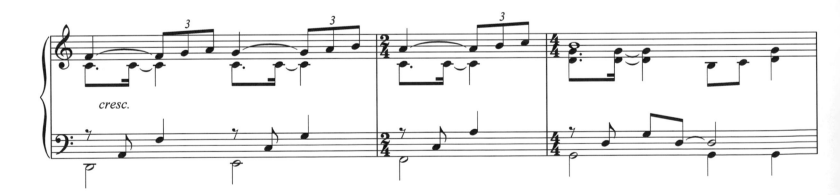

More broadly

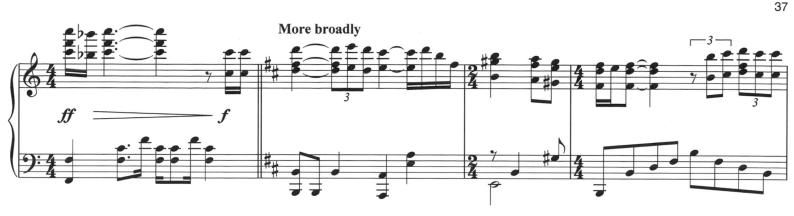

THE IMPERIAL MARCH
(Darth Vader's Theme)
from STAR WARS: THE EMPIRE STRIKES BACK

Music by JOHN WILLIAMS

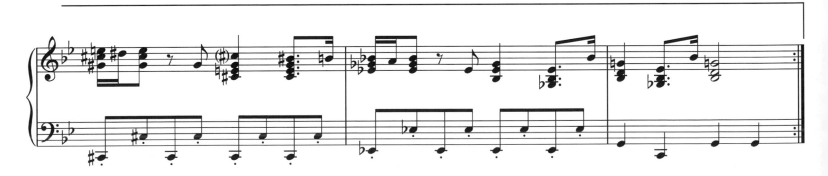

PRINCESS LEIA'S THEME

from STAR WARS: A NEW HOPE

Music by JOHN WILLIAMS

With a gentle flow

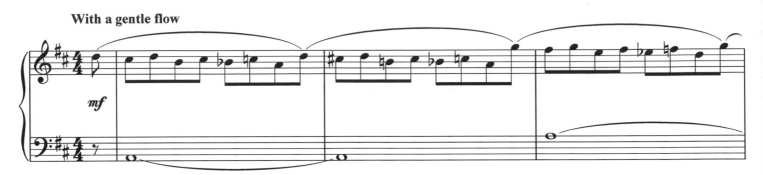

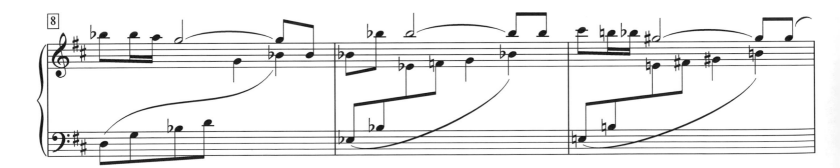

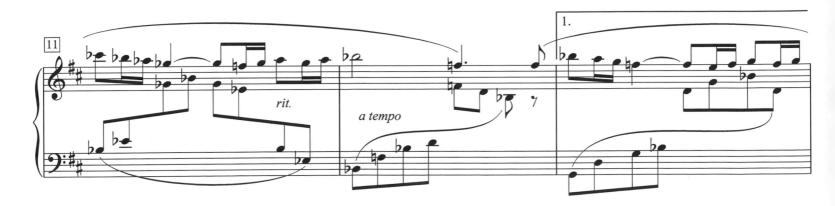

THEME FROM "STAR TREK®"

from the Paramount Television Series STAR TREK

Words by GENE RODDENBERRY
Music by ALEXANDER COURAGE

Bright Galactic Beguine

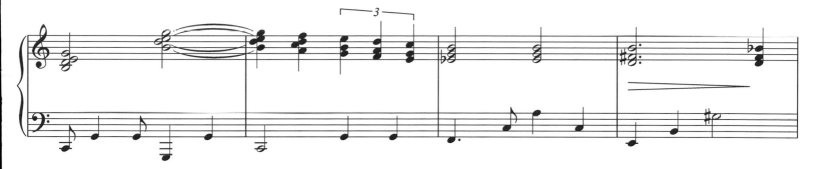

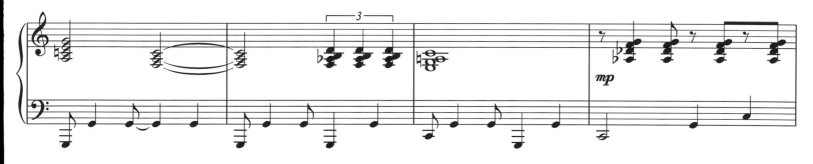

STAR TREK®: INSURRECTION
Theme from the Paramount Motion Picture STAR TREK: INSURRECTION

By JERRY GOLDSMITH

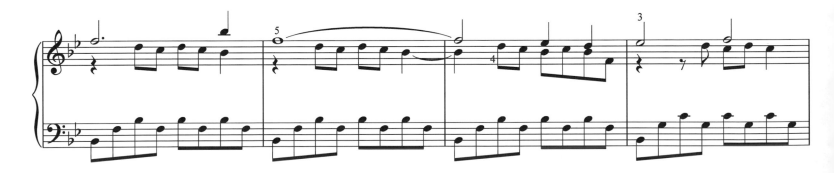

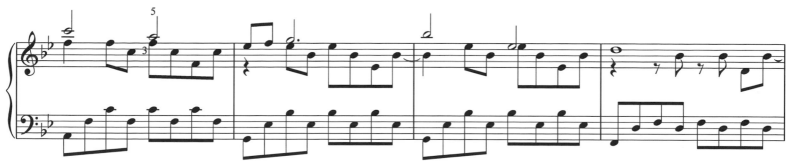

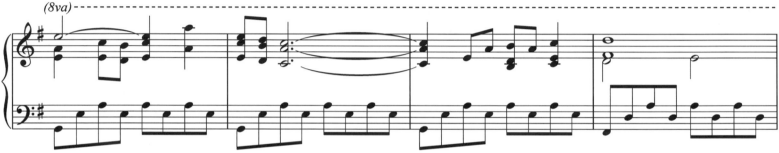

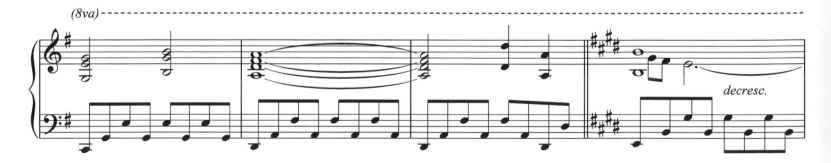

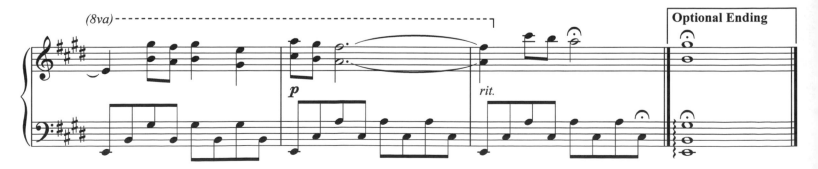

STAR WARS
(Main Theme)
from STAR WARS: A NEW HOPE

Music by JOHN WILLIAMS

Majestically, steady March (♩ = 108)

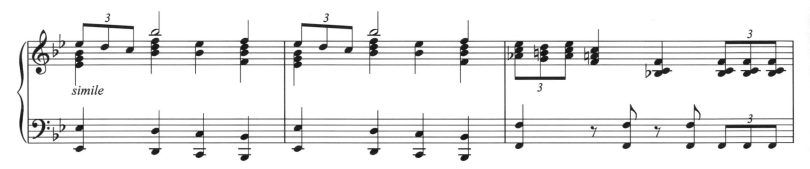

simile

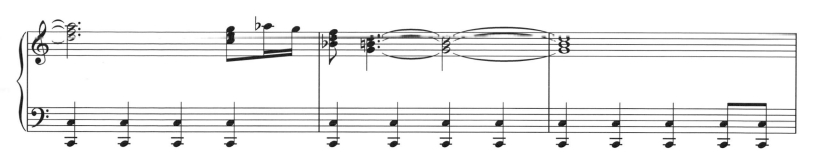

simile

STAR TREK® THE MOTION PICTURE

Theme from the Paramount Picture STAR TREK: THE MOTION PICTURE

Music by JERRY GOLDSMITH

Moderately fast March tempo

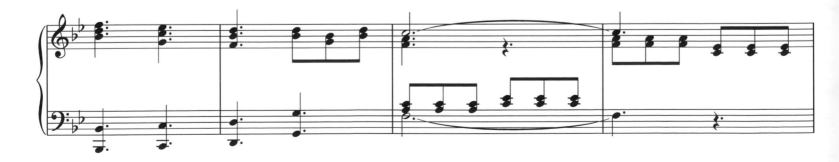

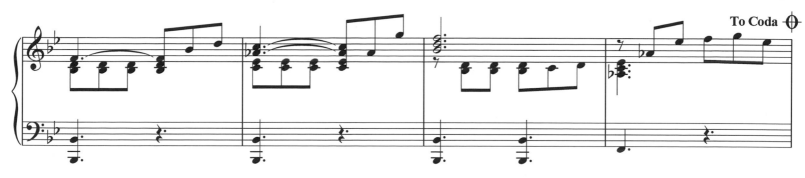

CODA

(♩. = ♩) **Slowly, expansively**

With pedal

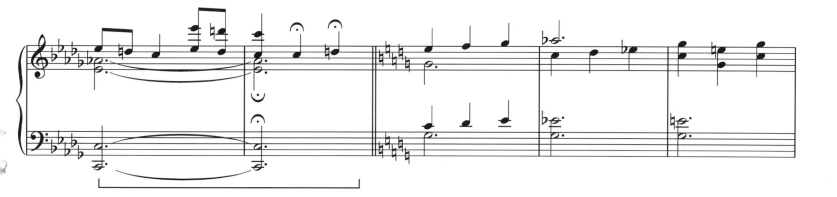

Tempo I

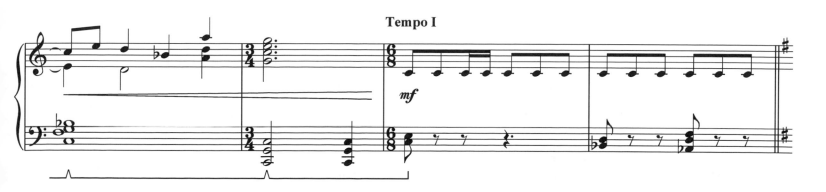

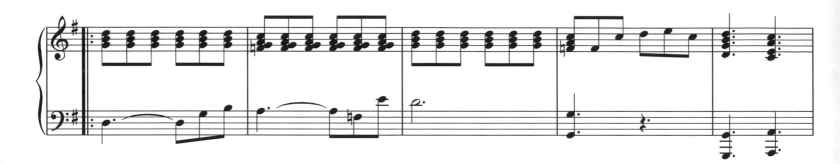

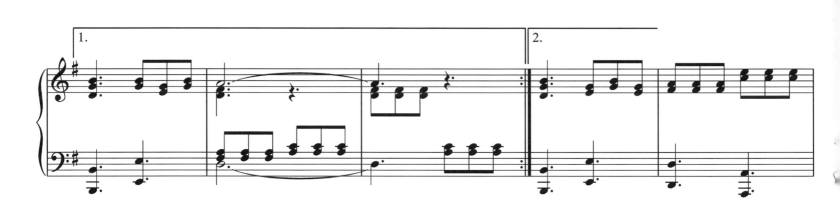

YOUR FAVORITE MUSIC
ARRANGED FOR PIANO SOLO

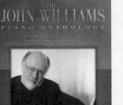

ARTIST, COMPOSER, TV & MOVIE SONGBOOKS

**Adele for Piano Solo –
3rd Edition**
00820186.............................. $19.99

The Beatles Piano Solo
00294023.............................. $17.99

**A Charlie Brown
Christmas**
00313176.............................. $19.99

**Paul Cardall –
The Hymns Collection**
00295925.............................. $24.99

Coldplay for Piano Solo
00307637.............................. $17.99

**Selections from
Final Fantasy**
00148699.............................. $19.99

**Alexis Ffrench – The
Sheet Music Collection**
00345258.............................. $19.99

Game of Thrones
00199166.............................. $19.99

Hamilton
00354612.............................. $19.99

**Hillsong Worship
Favorites**
00303164.............................. $14.99

How to Train Your Dragon
00138210.............................. $22.99

Elton John Collection
00306040.............................. $24.99

La La Land
00283691.............................. $16.99

John Legend Collection
00233195.............................. $17.99

Les Misérables
00290271.............................. $22.99

Little Women
00338470.............................. $19.99

Outlander: The Series
00254460.............................. $19.99

**The Peanuts®
Illustrated Songbook**
00313178.............................. $29.99

**Astor Piazzolla –
Piano Collection**
00285510.............................. $19.99

**Pirates of the Caribbean –
Curse of the Black Pearl**
00313256.............................. $22.99

Pride & Prejudice
00123854.............................. $17.99

Queen
00289784.............................. $19.99

John Williams Anthology
00194555.............................. $24.99

George Winston Piano Solos
00306822.............................. $22.99

MIXED COLLECTIONS

**Beautiful Piano
Instrumentals**
00149926.............................. $19.99

**Best Jazz
Piano Solos Ever**
00312079.............................. $27.99

**Big Book of
Classical Music**
00310508.............................. $24.99

Big Book of Ragtime Piano
00311749.............................. $22.99

Christmas Medleys
00350572.............................. $16.99

Disney Medleys
00242588.............................. $19.99

Disney Piano Solos
00313128.............................. $17.99

Favorite Pop Piano Solos
00312523.............................. $17.99

Great Piano Solos
00311273.............................. $19.99

**The Greatest Video
Game Music**
00201767.............................. $19.99

Most Relaxing Songs
00233879.............................. $19.99

**Movie Themes
Budget Book**
00289137.............................. $14.99

**100 of the Most Beautiful
Piano Solos Ever**
00102787.............................. $29.99

100 Movie Songs
00102804.............................. $32.99

Peaceful Piano Solos
00286009.............................. $19.99

**Piano Solos for
All Occasions**
00310964.............................. $24.99

Sunday Solos for Piano
00311272.............................. $17.99

Top Hits for Piano Solo
00294635.............................. $16.99

HAL•LEONARD®
View songlists online and order from your
favorite music retailer at
halleonard.com

Disney characters and artwork TM & © 2021 Disney